# Skiing

Clive
Gifford

WAYLAND

Published in Great Britain in 2015 by Wayland
First published in 2010

Dewey number: 796.9'3-dc22
ISBN: 978 0 7502 8894 1

10 9 8 7 6 5 4 3 2 1

Wayland
An imprint of Hachette Children's Group
Part of Hodder & Stoughton
Carmelite House
50 Victoria Embankment
London EC4Y 0DZ

Senior editor: Debbie Foy
Designer: Rebecca Painter
Photographer: Cindy Kleh

Acknowledgements:
The author and publisher would like to thank the following people for
participating in our photoshoot: Nic Seemann, Sydnie Kroneberger,
Patrick O'Connell, Elizabeth O'Connell, Hava Rohloff, Max Williams and
Storm Klomhaus.

A special thank you to Winter Park Resort, Colorado, US.

Photography by Cindy Kleh except:
5 top Getty Images; 7 bottom image courtesy of Chill Factor^e,
Manchester; 28 FRANCK FIFE/AFP/Getty Images; 29 top FRANCK
FIFE/AFP/Getty Images; 29 bottom JED JACOBSOHN/Getty Images

Printed in China

An Hachette UK Company

www.hachette.co.uk

www.hachettechildrens.co.uk

# Contents

# The world of skiing

Skiing is a way of moving across snow using long, flat runners called skis fitted to boots. It has become the most popular winter leisure pursuit in the world. Skiers can gently glide through wonderful winter scenery or travel fast down slopes testing their skills, balance and reactions. It's a sport to suit everyone!

## Different sports

Skiing has developed into a group of different competitive sports. Traditionally there were two types of skiing – **alpine** and **Nordic**. Alpine skiing is mostly downhill skiing with timed runs. Nordic skiing is mostly cross-country with skiers gliding along relatively flat trails. **Freestyle** skiing is becoming increasingly popular. Freestyle sees competitors perform spectacular moves or routines with judges marking their performances.

*A freestyle skier performs a move high in the air.*

## Skiing history

Long ago, skiing was used as an effective way of moving around on snow in colder regions. Archaeologists have unearthed early wooden skis from Iceland, Sweden, Norway and Finland – some are over 4,000 years old. From the fifteenth century, soldiers used skis to travel in Russia, Poland and Scandinavia. The earliest ski competitions were cross-country races, held in Norway in 1843, and downhill races in California in the 1860s. People began to go on ski holidays to Switzerland in the 1900s and, in 1924, the first Winter Olympics was held in France.

Nineteenth century Russian soldiers ski into battle.

Skiing is for everyone. This blind skier has a guide to help him on the slopes.

## Adaptive skiing

People with disabilities can ski using special ski equipment. Wheelchair-bound athletes can use short poles and a sit-ski – a type of shaped seat that glides over snow. Other skiers with disabilities may use outriggers which are ski poles with short skis on the bottom. Ski competitions for elite athletes with disabilities are increasingly popular with the best skiers taking part in the Winter Paralympics.

# Getting started

Your first ski experience might be close to home or on a skiing holiday. If you are not lucky enough to live in an area with regular snowfall there are a number of options including dry ski slopes, indoor snow domes and ski resorts.

## Ski resorts

Thousands of ski resorts all over the world welcome ski holiday makers. Some are world famous, such as Aspen in Colorado, St Moritz in Switzerland and Chamonix in France, but as a beginner all you need is a resort with gentle runs known as beginner or **nursery slopes**. These are low slopes with no obstructions and are perfect for learning basic ski skills.

*Learning to ski is a great challenge, but fun and exciting. Many beginners learn at ski schools in groups.*

## Artificial slopes

Many beginners use artificial slopes to get a first taste of skiing. Dry slope surfaces are made of plastic matting, often with a thin layer of water running across them to help **simulate** real snow slopes. Dry slopes are often found in mild climates so you may not need layers of warm clothing. However, the surface can be hard to fall on, so it's best to wear protective trousers, gloves, jacket and helmet. These are usually available for hire at the dry ski centre.

*Young skiers kitted out in helmets and jackets, admire the view at a US ski resort.*

## Skiing indoors

The world's first major indoor ski slope opened in Australia in 1987. Since then, many others have been built, mostly in countries with few or no ski resorts like the UK, Dubai and the Netherlands. The Chill Factor$^e$ in Manchester is the UK's largest indoor slope at 180 m (600 ft) long. Ski Dubai has a 400-m (1,300-ft) ski run, while Snowworld Landgraaf in the Netherlands boasts a 500-m (1,640-ft) ski slope.

## Ski school

Whether you are starting out on a dry slope, indoor slope or a major resort, the best way to start is to take lessons at a ski school. Experienced ski teachers can demonstrate basic techniques and identify mistakes in your stance or movements. Follow your teacher's instructions closely and you will improve.

*Used to boost outdoor snow levels or to generate snow at indoor ski slopes, snow cannon mix air and water to pump out artificial snow!*

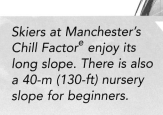

*Skiers at Manchester's Chill Factor$^e$ enjoy its long slope. There is also a 40-m (130-ft) nursery slope for beginners.*

# Get into the gear!

There are many ski clothing brands, styles and outfits to consider but the most important thing is that they fit well, and they are windproof and waterproof. For your first visit to a dry ski slope, a snow dome or a weekend at a ski resort, you do not need a whole ski wardrobe. Look to borrow items from other skiers or hire them from where you intend to ski.

## Layered clothing

Skiers keep warm by wearing three or more layers of clothing. The layers trap warm air which helps **insulate** you against cold conditions. The base layer is usually close-fitting thermal underwear that helps carry sweat away from your skin. The middle insulating layer is often a fleece or jumper. For the waterproof outer layer, skiers usually wear thick padded ski pants and jacket.

*Four layers of clothing will keep this skier warm for a day on the slopes.*

## Head, fingers and toes

A helmet is an essential part of your ski wear and should be fitted by an expert to help prevent injury on the slopes. Your extremities – your hands and feet – feel the cold the most, so keeping them warm is essential. Ski gloves are waterproof with a warm lining or a removable inner glove. For beginners, gloves are recommended over mitts as you can keep them on while adjusting clothing or equipment.

*A ski helmet is essential to protect you against injury. Goggles will protect your eyes against snow, sun glare and driving winds.*

## Storing kit

Ski pants or jackets usually feature zipped pockets to store small items such as keys, **sunblock** and a cereal bar or similar snack. Skiers out at a resort all day will often carry juice or water, further food and other items in a belted bag around their waist or in a small backpack.

*Ski glove cuffs overlap with your jacket to fully cover your wrists even when you stretch out your arms.*

*Neck gaiters are useful for keeping chilly winds at bay.*

*Ski socks are long and warm. Make sure they fit well and comfortably.*

## Stretching for skiing

Skiing is strenuous and can put strain on your major muscles. Before skiing, always spend ten minutes stretching your lower back, shoulders, groin and leg muscles. Stretching should be gentle, with no jerks or lurches, and each stretch should be held for a count of ten before repeating. This will help prevent muscle pulls or tears, which could halt your skiing adventure!

*This skier holds his arm across his chest for ten seconds to stretch his shoulder muscles.*

*Holding his heels and leaning back, this skier stretches his upper chest muscles.*

# Skis, boots and bindings

Ski boots support your feet and ankles. These attach to the skis with a clip mechanism called a ski binding. When starting out, your ski school manager will choose the correct size and type of boot, ski and binding for your size and age.

## Ski types

There are different types of ski depending on your ability. Beginners' alpine skis, for instance, are shorter than those used by experienced skiers. This makes them slower on the slopes but easier to control. Skis are made from a range of materials, from woods to polyurethane plastics. The bottom edges of skis are often finished in steel to resist **abrasion** and to help cut through the snow.

*Tip*

*Shovel* – the widest part of the ski and is crucial to turning.

*Waist* – the narrowest part of the ski where you place your boot.

*Base* – this is the underside of the ski.

*Binding toe*

*Ski brake*

*Binding heel piece*

*Tail*

## Boots and bindings

Your boot holds your foot at the correct forward angle when skiing. They should fit comfortably and you should be able to wiggle your toes and lift your heel, just slightly, inside the boot. Bindings anchor the ski boot to the ski and help absorb some of the shocks you feel when skiing. Bindings are designed to release your boot when you fall. Your ski school manager will adjust your bindings and it's important that you do not alter them or they may not work correctly.

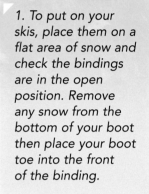

1. To put on your skis, place them on a flat area of snow and check the bindings are in the open position. Remove any snow from the bottom of your boot then place your boot toe into the front of the binding.

2. With your boot centred over the ski, press down firmly on the heel part of your binding. Your boot is fixed when the binding clicks into place.

## Waxing skis

Ski undersides can be coated with wax to reduce friction between the ski and the snow, helping them glide more easily. Different waxes are used for different types of skiing and snow conditions. Some waxes are sprayed on, while others are heated first with a ski waxer or applied with an iron.

**Strap** – loops around the wrist so that you don't lose your poles.

**Grip** – enables skiers to hold them comfortably.

## Ski poles

Ski poles are used for balance and turning. To check they are the right height, hold your pole just below its basket and rest the other end on the ground. Your lower arm should be parallel to the ground.

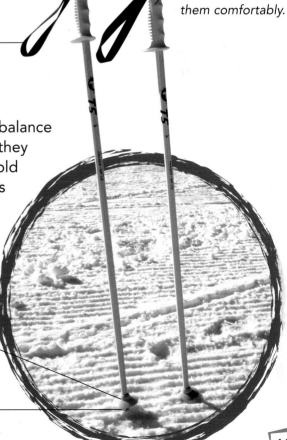

**Basket** – helps prevent the pole sinking too far into the snow.

**Tip** – enters the snow to help balance the skier.

# On the slopes

Your first visit to an outdoor ski resort is exciting – but there's plenty to take in! There are many signs, rules and different areas to ski. Read up on the resort and look at the resort map beforehand to learn about local rules and signs.

## On- and off-piste

Ski resorts usually have several marked-out ski runs or **pistes**. A piste is a slope that has been carefully prepared by the ski resort. When you start out, you will spend all your time on the beginner slopes. These are very gentle pistes usually with large **outrun** areas at the bottom. Off-piste skiing carries risk as the snow hasn't been prepared and might hide a **crevasse** or rocky outcrop that could cause injury. Off-piste skiing should only be performed by highly experienced skiers, often accompanied by a local guide.

*Check the resort map to find colour-coded pistes, location of ski lifts, medical centres and SOS telephones – if you find yourself in difficulty.*

*These skiers are about to ski a green run – especially suited to beginners.*

*This sign indicates a black run, with steep, fast slopes and obstacles such as rocks and trees.*

## Piste signs

Pistes are colour coded according to their speed and degree of difficulty. In Europe and the United States, the easiest, most gentle runs are coded green on signs and maps, and the hardest runs (only suitable for advanced skiers) are coded black. Make sure you only ski on runs that are suitable for your ability and experience.

## Ski lifts

Lifts provide you with the transport you need to get to the top of a slope. There are many different types but they are divided into **aerial lifts** and **surface lifts**. Chair lifts, trams and gondolas are types of aerial lift that carry you like a cable car above the slope. Surface lifts such as T-bar lifts, poma lifts and magic carpets tow, drag or carry you uphill on the surface of the slope.

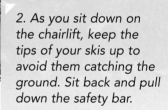

*1. As the chairlift approaches, hold both poles in one hand and steady the chair with your other hand.*

*2. As you sit down on the chairlift, keep the tips of your skis up to avoid them catching the ground. Sit back and pull down the safety bar.*

*This skier grips the pole of a poma lift. At the end of the pole is a plastic disc which goes behind the skier's legs.*

*A magic carpet is a sort of conveyor belt that skiers step onto to travel up beginner slopes.*

# Get moving!

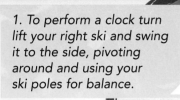

*1. To perform a clock turn lift your right ski and swing it to the side, pivoting around and using your ski poles for balance.*

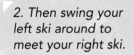

*2. Then swing your left ski around to meet your right ski.*

**Getting to grips with your ski equipment and learning to manoeuvre yourself around on skis is best learned on level ground or on gentle, rolling slopes.**

## Getting orientated

Beginners at a ski school will be shown simple exercises to get used to wearing skis, handling poles and keeping their balance. These include lifting one ski up at a time, sliding each ski back and forth along the snow and twisting at the knee to feel the ski edge dig into the snow. Beginners learn the correct way to 'walk' on skis and to pivot around to perform **clock turns** to change direction.

## Sidestepping

Alpine skis offer little grip so getting uphill is not easy! Side stepping is a technique you can use to move short or medium distances uphill.

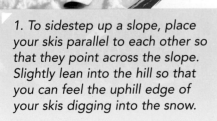

*2. Lift your upper ski and take small steps up the slope. Use your poles for support. Get your body weight over your upper ski then lift and step up with the lower ski. Repeat the steps smoothly and slowly, aiming to keep your balance.*

*1. To sidestep up a slope, place your skis parallel to each other so that they point across the slope. Slightly lean into the hill so that you can feel the uphill edge of your skis digging into the snow.*

## Ski stance

While skiing, a skier adjusts their body and leg position to speed up, slow down or make turns. They perform these movements and changes in position from a basic ski stance – the stance you would use if you were gliding forward on your skis in a straight line. Remember to keep your arms and legs bent slightly and your weight balanced between your two legs. This stance should feel relaxed and comfortable as you may be in this position for long periods during a busy day's skiing!

*Look in the direction you are heading – not down at your skis.*

*Upper body relaxed but upright. Don't let your bottom 'sag'.*

*Arms forward a little and bent at the elbows.*

*Knees bent so they are positioned over your toes.*

*Feet slightly apart but skis kept parallel to each other.*

## The herringbone

The herringbone is another type of uphill movement, usually used over short distances or for more gentle slopes.

*2. As one ski grips the snow, lift the other ski and take a small step forward up the slope. Use your poles for support.*

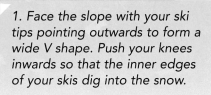

*1. Face the slope with your ski tips pointing outwards to form a wide V shape. Push your knees inwards so that the inner edges of your skis dig into the snow.*

# Making your first runs

During their first runs down a slope, skiers learn to understand the concept of the fall line. This is the quickest, most direct route down a slope. The closer your ski tips point down a fall line, the faster you will travel. Your first run may be a 'schuss' down a very gentle beginner slope. On steeper or longer runs, you will need to learn how to brake and turn.

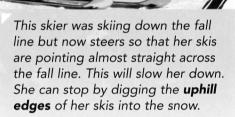

*fall line*

This skier was skiing down the fall line but now steers so that her skis are pointing almost straight across the fall line. This will slow her down. She can stop by digging the **uphill edges** of her skis into the snow.

## Schussing

Skiing straight down the **fall line** is called **schussing**. You start with your skis across the fall line and then take small steps to point your ski tips down the fall line. Try to stay relaxed and balanced equally over both skis as the skis and the slope do the work and take you down the slope at a gentle speed. As you come to a stop you can use your ski poles to balance you. As your schussing improves, you will learn how to bend and straighten your legs to absorb the shocks on bumps or dips you encounter on the slope.

*Relax your body into the basic stance, with knees, ankles and elbows bent.*

*Skis should be parallel, about the width of your hips.*

*Point your ski tips down the fall line.*

Schussing down a gentle slope, this skier is looking straight ahead, checking the terrain and watching out for other skiers.

## The snowplough

The **snowplough** is the simplest technique used to control your speed on a slope. It involves you pointing your ski tips towards each other and pushing the tails out to form a V shape. This will slow you down and can be adjusted by increasing or decreasing the width of the V shape and by pressing down more or less on the inside edges of the skis. When you start out, combining the snowplough with schussing will allow you to build up experience of simple runs and changing speeds as well as allowing you to work on your stance and balance.

*Schussing down a slope, the skier decides to slow down.*

*She starts to turn her ski tips inwards with the aim of performing a snowplough.*

*She brings the tips of her skis inwards until they are about 10 cm (4 in) apart and moves the rear of the skis outwards.*

## Snowplough turns

The snowplough technique can be adapted to perform a simple turn. First, snowplough down the fall line and then, to perform a turn to your right, get your head over your left ski and use your knee and foot to push gently against your left ski. You should feel its edge entering the snow while your right ski stays flat on the snow. Keeping your hips over both skis, you will find yourself veering off in a gentle curve to your right.

*She comes to a stop by digging the inside edges of her skis into the snow.*

# Traversing and turning

You can make a number of gentle and enjoyable runs through schussing and using the snowplough as a brake. But to tackle steeper slopes, you need to master a number of different techniques.

## Traversing

**Traversing** is crossing the fall line but with your skis parallel to each other. This allows you to travel faster than if you were performing a snowplough where you are braking constantly. Practise traversing at different speeds. If you find your speed building too much, move into the snowplough position to slow down.

*When traversing, bend your knees and keep your upper ski (the ski furthest up the slope) slightly forward of the lower ski.*

## Stem turns

Stemming is when the tail of one or both skis is pushed outwards from the skier. To perform a stem turn, the outside ski – the ski furthest from the centre of your turn – is stemmed just like it would be in a snowplough but the other ski is not. The outer ski will gently lead you into the turn and as you do, you plant your pole beside your lower ski, about halfway between the ski tip and your boot. You push against the outside ski, keeping on its edge as you turn first down and then round the slope.

*This skier stems her right ski as she eases into a stem turn.*

## Parallel turns

Most new skiers need to work their way up to **parallel turns**. Throughout the turn, the skis are kept parallel to each other so that your speed decreases less than with snowplough or stem turns. Parallel turning requires a skier to time their movements carefully. As you traverse, the uphill edges of your skis are digging into the snow. To parallel turn, you need to switch edges so that the lower edges of both skis connect with the snow. You do this by unweighting your skis – this means stretching your legs so that you grow taller and more upright. This will flatten your skis out.

You can then roll your skis into the turn. As you extend your legs, you also plant your inside pole in the snow which helps you turn round.

Once out of a parallel turn you can go back into traversing across a slope, ready to make another parallel turn the other way a short while later.

# Building experience

As with most things, practise makes perfect! As you progress, you will perform basic techniques without thinking, giving you more time to concentrate on choosing good routes, known as lines, across and down a slope.

*Skiing on freshly fallen powder snow is great fun and allows you to work on your turns and moves in soft snow.*

## Know your snow

Different types of snow can affect the way you ski. Here are the three main snow types:

- **Powder** is the name given to a surface covered in new snow that tends to be good for skiing.

- Crud is fresh powder that has been trampled down by skiers and snowboarders travelling the slopes. You need to ski carefully to allow for the uneven ride in places where snow has either been packed down or piled up.

- Soup or slush is wet, sticky snow that occurs in warmer conditions. Skiing on slush tends to be slow and turning needs more effort, but skiers need to be aware of hitting a patch of faster snow or ice.

## Staying alert

Pistes at major ski resorts are usually groomed regularly by machines. However, many pistes contain gentle rises and falls, and smaller bumps, mounds and ruts can form where others have skied before. All these things plus the possibility of a skier falling or slowing up ahead of you are why you must stay alert with your head up, eyes scanning your route ahead.

*A freshly groomed slope, prepared by a special grooming machine at many ski resorts.*

## Rises and falls

Skiers use their knees and legs as shock absorbers, rising up (or extending) and hunching down (or flexing) to ride over **moguls**, bumps and dips, while keeping balanced and on course. Whatever your manoeuvre aim to keep your back straight and your head up all the while.

*1. When approaching a mogul relax your knees slightly.*

*2. Bend them further as you go across the mogul.*

*3. Start to straighten up as you come down the other side and prepare to carry on skiing.*

## Side-slipping

**Side-slipping** is controlled sliding along the fall line of the slope. This is performed with your skis at right angles to the fall line and is useful to help you build your experience of using the edges of your skis.

# Ski safety

Skiing is a sport that comes with risks. You can cut down on these by skiing in good conditions, checking your equipment thoroughly and following a ski resort's safety rules.

## Climate conditions

Conditions when skiing outdoors can change dramatically. It can feel hot when the sun is out, but sudden strong winds and cloud cover can make temperatures drop significantly. Always dress warmer than you think necessary – you can always unzip your jacket to cool down. Be aware of the weather conditions and however much you want to ski, stop and return to base if heavy snowstorms or fog and mists look likely. Stay alert for avalanche warnings and never ski a piste that has been closed – often shown by yellow and black signs.

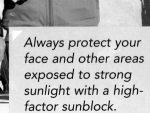

*Always protect your face and other areas exposed to strong sunlight with a high-factor sunblock.*

## Avoiding accidents

Ski slopes can be crowded places. Stay aware of others around you and, if you want to travel across a piste, check the way is clear. Never ski too close to others and if you want to overtake a slower skier, it is your responsibility to do this safely. Accidents are more likely to happen when you are tired. **Fatigue** tends to make you less alert and less able to control your body and skis. If you are tired, take a rest and remember to drink plenty to top up your fluid levels.

*Major ski resorts usually have a medical centre and piste patrols that travel around the slopes looking to help injured skiers. If you see someone injured, stop and offer help. Do not move an injured person but try to phone for help as soon as possible.*

*One skier has gone for help, while another stays with someone who has fallen and has suffered an injury. They have marked their position with crossed skis in the snow.*

## Hypothermia

If you have not dressed warmly or taken note of a sudden drop in temperature, there is a threat of hypothermia. This is a dangerous condition where the body's temperature falls below 35°C. A person suffering from hypothermia may show signs of feeling confused, shivering uncontrollably with slow, shallow breathing. Getting medical help is a priority.

# Alpine competition skiing

Alpine ski racing is hugely popular in Europe and further afield – involving downhill, slalom, giant slalom and Super-G races.

## The downhill

This is the fastest and one of the most popular of all major alpine skiing competitions. Skiers race down a course, usually three or so kilometres (2 miles) long, containing steep slopes and drops. The total **drop** on a course must be 800–1,100 m (2,600–3,600 ft) for men and 500–800 m (1,640–2,600 ft) for women. Skis for downhill are longer than those used in other alpine races and ski poles are bent to fit around the body which helps cut down air resistance. These, a close-fitting ski suit and a tucked-in racing stance can help skiers reach speeds of over 150 km/h (93 mph).

*A downhill skier, wearing a competition vest over her ski suit, races down a course. She uses the edge of her skis to keep control as she turns.*

## Slalom

The ski slalom is a test of turning skills, speed and control. A skier has to turn almost continuously as they ski through a long series of **gates**. Skiers are allowed to knock the gates (which are hinged to avoid injury) on their way down the slalom course and try to build a good rhythm for the quickest possible time.

*There are around 50-75 gates on a course, coloured alternately red and blue. Slalom skiers have to pass through all of the gates or face disqualification.*

## Giant slalom and Super-G

These two events combine the skills required in slalom along with the sheer speed found in downhill. A giant slalom course contains 50 or more gates but spread out over a longer distance on a steeper slope than the slalom. It is a tremendous test of a skier's strength, stamina and technical skill. A Super-G course has fewer gates but the course is steeper and speeds faster.

*This skier competes in a Super-G competition, performing a single run down a long, fast course which has at least 30 gates for women and 35 for men.*

## Parallel slalom

Regular slalom races are timed against the clock but parallel slalom events are head-to-head competitions. Two skiers ski identical courses side by side, making two runs, with the overall winner progressing to the next round.

# Cross-country and freestyle skiing

Millions of people enjoy other forms of skiing aside from alpine. Cross-country (or Nordic) skiing is hugely popular with skiers of all ages, and freestyle skiing is attracting a cool following of advanced young skiers.

## Cross-country skiing

Many skiers enjoy cross-country skiing on prepared tracks found at many skiing resorts. Cross-country skis are long and thin, designed to grip the snow and glide along it. Skiers use different walking and gliding techniques to increase speed or to keep moving but conserve energy. The double pole push, for example, is used to speed up movement over relatively level ground. Both poles are planted just ahead of the skier's body before the skier pushes off the poles at the same time. Some techniques, such as side-stepping to climb uphill, are used in both cross-country and alpine skiing.

## Cross-country competitions

There are many cross-country events from short 1 km (0.6 mile) sprints to long-distance races which at the Olympics are 20–30 km (12–18 miles) long for women and 50 km (31 miles) long for men. Away from the Olympics, ultra long-distance marathons can be over 100 km (62 miles), while an event called the Nordic Combined features both a cross-country race and a ski jump competition.

*Cross-country skis are designed for gliding easily over the snow. The basic technique combines walking and gliding in an easy rhythmic series of movements.*

## Freestyle skiing

Freestyle is the name given to a group of skiing disciplines including **aerials** and moguls that more experienced skiers can take part in for fun or competition. Freestyle aerial skiers launch themselves off ramps and jumps. Once high in the air, they perform spectacular tricks and moves including somersaults and twists. Their jump, tricks in the air and landing are all awarded a score by a panel of judges.

Moguls are large bumps in the snow that can form naturally or be shaped to form a **mogul run**. Skiers can work on their cross-country skills skiing down a mogul run and avoiding the bumps. In competitions, skiers perform tricks such as back flips and twists as they navigate a mogul run which includes small jumps known as kickers.

*A freestyle skier performs a great aerial move crossing his skis in mid-air.*

*Top aerial skiers can perform triple somersaults or four complete twists through the air on a single jump.*

## Terrain parks

Terrain parks are a snow-based version of skateboarding parks. They are marked off areas at a ski resort which contain a number of features built for freestyle skiers (as well as snowboarders) to enjoy. Some terrain park features are made from snow such as a mogul field full of rounded humps or a large, shallow bowl cut into deep snow. Other features are constructed park 'furniture' such as ramps and jumps and metal-edged rails and boxes, which skiers ride up and along (as this boy is doing in the picture shown here).

# Skiing around the world

Skiing competitions have been held all over the world for more than a century. The International Ski Federation (FIS) organises many different regional and world championships.

## World Championships

Cross-country skiing was the first to have its own world championships back in 1925, followed by alpine skiing in 1931. FIS World Championships are now held every two years at different major ski resorts around the world. The 2007 Nordic World Championships were held in Sapporo, Japan. In 2011, the Alpine World Championships are at Garmisch in Germany and the World Freestyles in Deer Valley in the US state of Utah.

US skier, Bode Miller skis down the men's slalom course at the 2009 World Ski Championships in Val d'Isere, France.

## The World Cup

For alpine skiing, the World Cup is a prestigious competition with massive live and television audiences. It is a series of races held in different locations in Europe, North America and, sometimes, Asia, every year. Skiers compete in slalom, downhill, Super-G, giant slalom and combined races. Trophies are awarded in each type of race but the biggest prize is the overall title as it is seen as the ultimate test of an alpine skier's ability. The most successful champions are Luxembourg's Marc Girardelli with five men's overall titles and Austria's Annemarie Moser-Pröll with six women's overall titles.

*Janica Kostelic from Croatia competes in the 2006 Olympics held in Torino, Italy.*

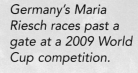

*Germany's Maria Riesch races past a gate at a 2009 World Cup competition.*

## The Winter Olympics

For many top skiers, the ultimate prize is to win a gold medal at the Winter Olympics. These are held every four years with the most recent competition hosted in Vancouver, Canada in 2010. The Winter Olympics features a range of winter sports from ice hockey to figure skating, but alpine, cross-country, freestyle aerial and mogul skiing are also important features of the games.

## Ski cross

Ski cross is a new and exciting skiing sport, considered part of freestyle skiing, which made its first Olympic appearance in 2010. In a ski cross race, between four and six skiers race at the same time over a tough technical course which features jumps, sloping turns, moguls and other obstacles. Skiers reach speeds of over 70km/h (47 mph) and the racing can be close and exciting for both skiers and spectators.

# Glossary

**Abrasion**   This is when something wears away due to being rubbed against something else.

**Aerials**   A type of freestyle skiing competition where competitors ski a ramp leading to high jumps, flips, twists and turns in the air.

**Aerial lift**   A way of travelling up a ski slope where the skier is lifted completely off the ground, such as in a chair lift.

**Alpine**   This refers to regular downhill skiing.

**Clock turns**   A way of turning on the spot by lifting a ski and turning in a circle.

**Crevasse**   A large, deep and often dangerous crack in a layer of snow and ice.

**Drop**   The distance (usually given in metres) straight downwards that a slope or piste runs. It helps give an idea of how steep the slope is.

**Fall line**   The straightest and steepest line down any slope.

**Fatigue**   Tiredness caused by the exercise that comes with skiing for a long period.

**Freestyle**   Acrobatic sports skiing that includes freestyle routines and skiing over moguls.

**Gate**   A series of hinged flags or poles through which skiers must ski between on the way down a slalom or other competition course.

**Insulate**   To surround your body with clothing to stop the heat you generate inside your body from escaping.

**Moguls**   Mounds of snow, both natural and skier made.

**Mogul run**   A slope full of bumps (or moguls) which are often caused by many skiers turning in the same place or are created deliberately for a competition.

**Nordic**   This refers to cross-country skiing.

**Nursery slopes**   Gentle and usually quite short slopes down which beginners make their first runs and learn basic techniques.

**Outrun**   A flat area at the bottom of the hill where skiers can come to a gradual stop.

**Parallel turn**   To change direction but keeping your skis parallel to each other throughout the turn.

**Piste**   A ski run which has been prepared by ski resort staff, pressing the snow down.

**Powder**   Freshly fallen snow which has not yet been compressed by skiers.

**Schussing**   To travel straight down a ski slope's fall line with the skis parallel to each other.

**Side-slipping**   A controlled, sideways slide down a slope.

**Simulate**   To pretend to be or mimic something else.

**Snowplough**   A basic ski position with the ski tips pointing inwards to form a V-shape and used to control a skier's speed.

**Sunblock**   A substance, usually a cream or lotion, that prevents the sun's harmful UV rays from causing sunburn.

**Surface lift**   A lift that pulls or carries skiers up a slope without lifting them off the ground.

**Traversing**   To ski across a slope at an angle to the fall line.

**Uphill edge**   The edge of the ski that is in a position higher up the slope.

# Further information

## Books to read

*Go Ski*, Warren Smith, Dorling Kindersley (2006)
A book with 30-minute DVD aimed at adults and older children and full of techniques and tips.

*Let's Go Skiing*, Peter Lawson, Brown Dog Books (2009)
Excellent first guide to skiing with lots of informative photographs.

*Skiing & Snowboarding: 52 Brilliant Ideas for Fun on the Slopes*, Cathy Struthers, Infinite Ideas Limited (2005)
A fun text guide full of useful tips to more enjoyable skiing.

## Useful contacts

*The International Ski Federation*
www.fis-ski.com

*The Ski Club of Great Britain*
www.skiclub.co.uk/skiclub/default.aspx

*Canadian ski clubs and organisation by province*
www.goski.ca/ski-Clubs.asp

*Ski and Snowboard Australia*
www.skiandsnowboard.org.au

## Websites

www.abc-of-skiing.com

*A great website with features on all aspects of skiing from basic techniques and choice of equipment to safety, exercises and resort tips.*

www.skicentral.com

*A useful resource with hundreds of links and pages on resorts, equipment and different forms of skiing.*

www.skimybest.com

*Another excellent collection of links to skiing websites divided into clubs, resorts, ski sports and other categories.*

www.olympic.org/uk

*Learn more about alpine skiing on the Olympic website.*

www.inawashiro2009.jp/english

*Visit the official website of the 2009 Freestyle Skiing World Championships to view action videos and photographs of competitors in action.*

# index